Psychodrama

Psychodrama

A Beginner's Guide

*Zoran Djurić, Jasna Veljković
and Miomir Tomić*

Jessica Kingsley Publishers
London and Philadelphia

First published in Serbian in 2003
by the Serbian Association of Psychologists.
First published in English in 2003 by Zoran Djurić.

This edition published in 2006 by
Jessica Kingsley Publishers
116 Pentonville Road
London N1 9JB, UK
and
400 Market Street, Suite 400
Philadelphia, PA 19106, USA

www.jkp.com

Library of Congress Cataloging in Publication Data
A CIP catalog record for this book is available from the Library of Congress

British Library Cataloguing in Publication Data
A CIP catalogue record for this book is available from the British Library

ISBN-13: 978 1 84310 411 7
ISBN-10: 1 84310 411 3

Printed and bound in China
by Amity Printing Co.,ltd.
APC-FT4145

CONTENTS

PREFACE

Early in the 20th century, Vienna was the stage for artistic and scientific developments with lasting international importance. In the ruins of the powerful Austro-Hungarian empire emerged the ideas and innovations of the psychotherapists Freud, Adler, Jung, the painters Kokoschka, Klimt and Schiele, the authors Weininger, Buber and Kafka, and the founder of group psychotherapy and psychodrama, Jacob Levi Moreno (1889–1974). It was in Vienna that Moreno, born to a Jewish merchant from Istanbul and a fourteen-year-old girl on a ship in the middle of the Black Sea, embarked on his existential and scientific adventure. He studied medicine and theology, found inspiration in the ideas of Martin Buber, the philosopher of dialogue, and continued from the point where Freud had stopped with his revelation of the power of the unconscious in man. It is not unconscious libidinal and aggressive energies that make the world go round, contended Moreno, but human encounter:

A meeting of two; eye to eye, face to face,
And when you are near I will tear your eyes out
and place them in place of mine,
and you will tear my eyes out
and will place them instead of yours,
then I will look at you with your eyes
and you will look at me with mine.

(From *Invitation to an Encounter*, 1915)

Moreno founded the Theatre of Spontaneity (Stegreiftheater), where he pursued his search for the Encounter. His wished for his epitaph to be, "J.L. Moreno: The man who brought laughter to psychotherapy."

WHAT IS PSYCHODRAMA?

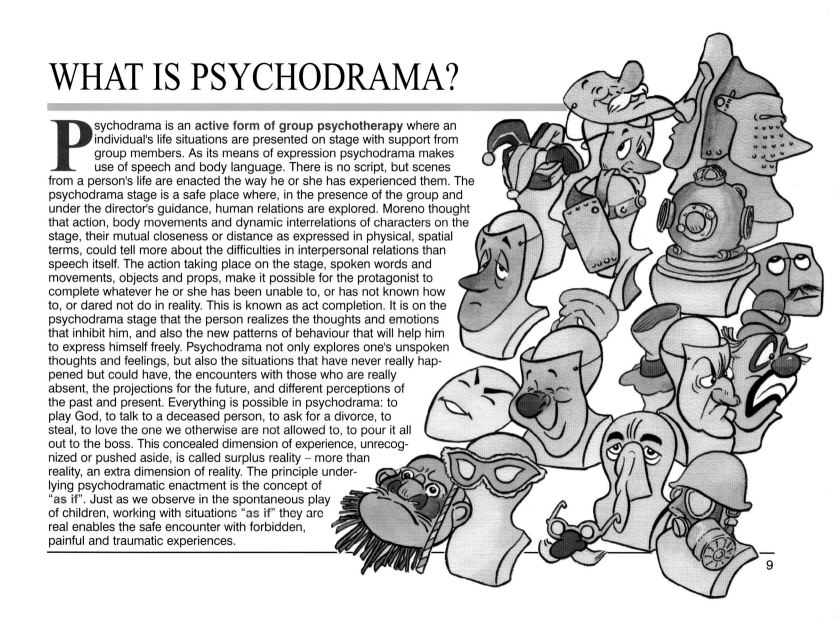

Psychodrama is an **active form of group psychotherapy** where an individual's life situations are presented on stage with support from group members. As its means of expression psychodrama makes use of speech and body language. There is no script, but scenes from a person's life are enacted the way he or she has experienced them. The psychodrama stage is a safe place where, in the presence of the group and under the director's guidance, human relations are explored. Moreno thought that action, body movements and dynamic interrelations of characters on the stage, their mutual closeness or distance as expressed in physical, spatial terms, could tell more about the difficulties in interpersonal relations than speech itself. The action taking place on the stage, spoken words and movements, objects and props, make it possible for the protagonist to complete whatever he or she has been unable to, or has not known how to, or dared not do in reality. This is known as act completion. It is on the psychodrama stage that the person realizes the thoughts and emotions that inhibit him, and also the new patterns of behaviour that will help him to express himself freely. Psychodrama not only explores one's unspoken thoughts and feelings, but also the situations that have never really happened but could have, the encounters with those who are really absent, the projections for the future, and different perceptions of the past and present. Everything is possible in psychodrama: to play God, to talk to a deceased person, to ask for a divorce, to steal, to love the one we otherwise are not allowed to, to pour it all out to the boss. This concealed dimension of experience, unrecognized or pushed aside, is called surplus reality – more than reality, an extra dimension of reality. The principle underlying psychodramatic enactment is the concept of "**as if**". Just as we observe in the spontaneous play of children, working with situations "**as if**" they are real enables the safe encounter with forbidden, painful and traumatic experiences.

WHO COMES TO PSYCHODRAMA?

People from all walks of life and all ages come to psychodrama. The method applies to anyone who wants to work out their fears and conflicts, or to change their relationships with other people. Psychodrama groups may be formed from people of approximately the same age or suffering from similar distress. In terms of activities they are engaged in, they range from high-school and university students to medical doctors and psychologists. Groups can function as therapeutic, educational or experiential. With respect to problems dealt with by their members, they may be composed of adolescents, married couples, patients or professionals engaged in any kind of activity. Eligible to join a group is anyone capable of controlling his aggressive and sexual impulses so as to avoid disturbance to others. Educational groups provide training for medical doctors, psychologists, teachers and people in related professions in order to help them improve their practice. As part of their personal development, they may work on their fears, conflicts or resistances in relation to their professional role.

Sessions usually last for about three hours, and ongoing groups may meet once or twice per week. The duration of groups is highly varied. Some groups work as long as it takes for the members to resolve their problems, which could be three to five years. Other groups are shorter term, where people can re-join as needed.

Participating in the group process helps each member to become aware of what he shares in common with other people, and also helps him to become aware of how to better relate with other people. Each member of the group is bound by agreements of confidentiality, respect and good will towards the other members of the group.

What does one lose with psychodrama?

Illusions about oneself and about others.

WHO IS THE PSYCHODRAMATIST?

The term psychodrama was coined from the words "**psyche**" – **soul** or mind, and "**drama**"– **action**. The psychodramatist is a group therapist directing the enactment of the protagonist's perceptions and life events while being assisted by the other group members. Psychodrama therapists are men and women who can communicate well and who are relaxed in their behaviour. They are skilful at establishing and maintaining communication, and are capable of sympathy while also maintaining correct professional boundaries. They are usually over thirty, because it is at about that age that they have managed to complete their studies and the additional training in psychodrama. The psychodramatist's work involves several roles: those of a **group therapist**, of an **analyst** and a **producer**. As a **therapist**, he helps the protagonist to initiate change, and facilitates and stimulates the therapeutic process. As an **analyst**, he points to the origin of the problem and to the connections in the protagonist and group's behaviour in various situations. As a **producer**, he initiates, shapes and organizes activities on the stage. In order to direct a psychodrama, the psychodramatist must possess the required skills.

PROFESSIONAL ROLES OF THE PSYCHODRAMATIST

ROLES	FUNCTIONS	SKILLS	IDEALS
THERAPIST	GIVING	UNDERSTANDING OF MIND AND BODY	SPONTANEITY
ANALYST	RECEIVING	SYMPATHY	CREATIVITY
TEACHER	EMPATHY	STAGING	GOOD HEALTH
GROUP LEADER	STIMULATION	DIRECTING	FREEDOM

R O L E S

THERAPIST
Helps
remove
distress and
psychological
problems

ANALYST
Discloses
the relation
between
here and now,
and then and
there

TEACHER
Teaches group
members to
think about
themselves,
to understand
themselves
and others

GROUP LEADER
Selects
members for
a group,
organizes
time and
space, and
directs
sessions

F U N C T I O N S

GIVING
Gives his
presence,
knowledge,
understanding
and support

RECEIVING
Receives
uneasiness, guilt
feelings, sorrow
and pain in
order to return
them alleviated
or seen under a
different light

EMPATHY
Ability to
imagine the
feelings of
other people
and respond
according to
their needs

STIMULATION
Points to
the ways
of resolving
problems

S K I L L S

UNDERSTAND-ING OF MIND AND BODY
Interprets
gestures, atti-
tudes of the
body, words,
facial expres-
sions etc.

SYMPATHY
Ability to
receive and
share in the
emotions of
others

STAGING
Sets the scene,
the concepts of
when and
where – every
situation is
defined by
characters,
time and place

DIRECTING
Warms up the
group and
leads it from
scene to scene
towards
sharing

I D E A L S

SPONTANEITY
Prerequisite
of creativity,
condition free
from anxiety

CREATIVITY
New response
to an old
situation and
adequate
response to a
new situation

GOOD HEALTH
Ability to be
spontaneous,
creative,
prepared for
change

FREEDOM
Uninhibited
energy,
spontaneity
and creativity

BASIC ELEMENTS OF PSYCHODRAMA

GROUP-AUDIENCE

In psychodrama sessions, all of the group members are involved; there is no designated "audience" and the protagonist is not the sole bearer of the action. The other members of the group enact diverse roles assigned to them by the protagonist and the director. The way they understand and sense a given psychodramatic situation contributes to the resolution of the protagonist's conflicts, but at the same time they gain insight into their own repressed or unrecognized thoughts and feelings.

To put it in modern terms, psychodrama is a kind of interactive theatre.

The protagonist is the initiator of action, but an encounter with the protagonist produces an energetic response from the members who enact the other roles, and from the director who makes every effort to ensure a spontaneous and creative progression of dramatic action. Sometimes the emotional response of the director and of the auxiliary egos – the group members in the roles of significant others – may significantly affect the development of action. The group-audience is always active. Its part appears closest to that of a theatre audience when, similarly to the chorus in ancient Greek drama, it resonates with the protagonist's experience or comments on it. Even then, the group is far more active than any theatrical audience who are watching and listening, laughing and worrying, getting thoughtful or bored, but never have the chance to intervene in the sequence of dramatic events the way it always comes about in psychodrama.

PROTAGONIST

In psychodrama, the protagonist is the person who presents in front of the group a situation from his life. Whether a patient, an educator, or just an individual willing to share his thoughts and feelings with others, and generous and open to the pain and suffering of others, he is always the hero of a human drama. In any person's life, there may be "unfinished business." Sometimes a thought of ours remains short of words, or an emotion played down, or we feel misunderstood, rejected, unhappy or, for some reason, guilty. Psychodrama gives us an opportunity to find this missing piece, to express what we have always wanted to but have not dared to do, to cry when we are sad or sing when we are happy. Unable in our real life to give free rein to our imagination, in psychodrama we can do that. All our hidden roles, untried possibilities, suppressed energies are given a chance on the stage to arise and reveal themselves to the full. An unfinished utterance, a choked-back thought, a swallowed word, a heart

WHERE DO YOU WANT TO GET WITH YOUR PSYCHODRAMA?

I WANT TO EXPLORE MY RELATIONSHIP WITH MY MOTHER

bursting at the seams with strong feelings – such fragments of a lost whole surface on the stage and are brought to consciousness (acting in), thereby receiving a context and meaning in relation to the significant Other. To experiment with fresh possibilities, give vent to imagination, start a conversation where there has never been one – all this enhances the choice of our roles, providing a guideline to our behaviour in the relationships and situations we consider important. With whom, where and when we have been left misread, reticent and sad – all of this we explore in our capacity as protagonist on stage.

DIRECTOR

Employing the technique of psychodrama, the group leader **guides the protagonist towards the resolution of his problem**. This resolution helps other members of the group resolve their problems, because the participation in a psychodramatic enactment arouses in group members strong feelings and associations with their own experience. The director helps the protagonist recreate scenes from his life on stage. He is attentive to the protagonist's feelings, **"emotional smoke"** and discourse, as well as to his own response to the psychodramatic action, in order to make it easier for the protagonist to attain mental catharsis. The group is often guided by two directors, a **co-therapeutic couple**. The latter situation amplifies and divides the group members' feelings for the therapists, and reminds them of their relationship to the parental couple in their own families. In educational groups, members may also function as directors.

AUXILIARY EGO

The auxiliary ego is a **group member playing the role of the significant Other, an important person from the protagonist's life**. The spouse, child, parents or friends are represented on the psychodrama stage in order to portray the protagonist's social atom. The professor, therapist, boss, political leader, or priest also appear as characters. According to their relevance to the protagonist, these are transference figures, the replicas of persons from the protagonist's social atom/primary family group. Support for the protagonist may also be provided by imagined characters, for example God, a fictional hero, or a rescuing 'knight in shining armour.' The protagonist often introduces, and the auxiliary ego takes, the role of a significant object, a chair, a bed or a picture, his room and other interiors where he has had some significant experience. Sometimes exploration focuses on the protagonist's relationship to a large group (a nation, state) of which he is a member, or on his conceptions of justice, faith, war, love or friendship. The auxiliary ego always acts as instructed by the protagonist: although entitled to play up a trait according to his own experience, to emphasize a word and

add a phrase, he must never go beyond the limits set by the protagonist's experience. In groups directed by a co-therapeutic couple one of the two often takes the role of the so-called trained auxiliary, an auxiliary ego acting out typified roles of the father, mother, president, neighbour. To act as a trained auxiliary ego requires familiarity with the socio-cultural pattern that the protagonist comes from. Sometimes, an auxiliary will take on the role of thc protagonist, and this is called a "**double**." The auxiliary who is opposing the protagonist is termed the "**antagonist**."

STAGE

The stage Moreno designed for this psychodramatic theatre was reminiscent of a wedding cake, each of its levels having a clearly defined purpose: one for daily life scenes, one for fantasy situations, and one where passions reigned. From the balcony spoke the untouchable, gods and judges. It was from the very form of the stage and from different occurrences on it that the spectator could get some idea of the protagonist's life and inner events.

Where an actual stage is not used, a portion of the group's working space, which may be a classroom, a lounge or even an outdoor area, is reserved for the stage. The **division of space must be clear and defined**: on one side are the chairs for group members, all of whom are aware of their being in real space and time. On the other side is the stage, where the protagonist's life scenes, which belong to an imagined time and space, are acted out. This is the place where the 'as if' enactment develops.

The props used on stage comprise light chairs and tables, and small easy-to-move objects that may stand for a bed, a wardrobe, a piano, and for other heavy items that a scene may require. Objects may also symbolize people. For scenes involving violent outbursts, elongated cylindrical cushions, soft fabrics or light plastic tubes may be used. Blows with such "weapons" cannot really cause pain or physical injury, while being convincing enough to sustain the make-believe of "as if" situations. It is essential to say that everyone on stage must be protected from physical or psychological harm. If the protagonist or auxiliary egos find themselves unable to enact a scene, some other way of exploring it is worked out.

PSYCHODRAMA

WARM-UP

Any piece of work to be done requires a warm-up, like a walk uphill. Warm-up is a gradual, goal-directed increase in physical and mental activity, and is a vital preparation for relating to other people. What moves us is the presence and mood of the other. Whether we are in opposition to or in accord with the other, the relationship, in the beginning, is never fully defined and recognized. It is only with the change of our mental state induced by conflicts in our relationship with the other person that we become aware of our own emotions, desires, thoughts and aspirations. Properly warmed-up, we can focus our attention on the relationship with the other person, embodied in a living person in front of us, or in a professional problem we are dealing with. Warmed-up, we are aware of the situation, we can think and feel, reason and comprehend, feel angry or cheerful, make choices and decisions, recognize the best course of action for ourselves and others. In other words, we are spontaneous, because our powers have been activated, and we are creative, because our actions change our attitude towards events and other people. Only when we are spontaneous and creative do we become present and fully ourselves in our being with others.

When leading a warm-up, the director assigns the group members any of a variety of tasks. For example: Walk as if you were happy, or sad. Or, imagine yourself flicking through a family album. Which photograph do you like best? Or, imagine that you are your favourite object. The purpose of such tasks is to arouse feelings and memory associations in group members. If the warm-up has triggered an experience, thought, feeling, memory or expectation, the group member is encouraged to link this with a situation from their life.

These warm-up tasks happen at times to be unnecessary. If the work in the previous session has been left unfinished, feelings in the group remain strong and questions plentiful. In such a case, the work resumes from the point of interruption, not necessarily with the same protagonist, but with unchanged emotions and problems.

The director also warms up. He keeps a close eye on the developments, and his mind wide open to receive the group's emotional vibrations. Well equipped for prompt recognition, processing and understanding, he decides on his mode of intervention: whether to concentrate on bringing the group as a whole to awareness, or to stimulate an individual flooded with strong feelings.

CHOICE OF PROTAGONIST

Having warmed up, the group take seats in a circle and share their experience. The protagonist is the group member who has been most strongly aroused by the warm-up. In case there are several potential protagonists, each of them proposes the underlying theme of his drama. Through a selection process group members eventually make their choice. It is not a democratic process in the political sense of the word. Nevertheless, every group has its "emotional policy", an unconscious process of sharing similar feelings. It is this unconscious contact between beings that decides preferences of members within a group for one another. That means that the protagonist never works for himself only, but always both for himself and for others. It is in the protagonist that lies the rub, the point of encounter and intersection of the emotional forces that exist within the group.

The protagonist may also be the director's choice. If he senses that someone in the group is experiencing strong feelings, he can simply invite the person to enter onto the stage and commence with his drama. Or he can take the future protagonist by the hand and lead him to the stage. However, this puts the therapist in a very powerful position. Consequently, he must be aware that, thereby, he has taken the attitude of someone superior to the protagonist, of someone who knows all there is to know, like a parent who knows what's best for the child. When the director takes the role of "the one who knows for others", "the group's emotional policy" is such that the main course of feelings becomes directed towards the director, who thus ceases being just a therapist and becomes the all-knowing and all-powerful charismatic leader of the group. That is something the leader of such a group must be acutely aware of. Which, after all, forms part of his warm-up and responsibility.

ACTION

The action starts with the protagonist's entrance onto the stage. His feelings and personal conflicts come out ever more clearly as the drama develops. The drama is a sequence of his life scenes and his internal events, fantasies and dreams enveloped in a common emotional state. What every drama hopes to achieve is to get to the core of the problem, to the protagonist's primary conflict. Both the director and group members come soon to realize that a single drama will not suffice to achieve the goal.

Once on stage, the protagonist specifies the issue he would like to deal with. He then makes a verbal agreement – sometimes called a "contract" – with the director and group. This may, for example, be formulated as follows: "I want to work on my relationship with my mother." This means that on that particular day he is ready to deal with that problem, and not with some other that may emerge during the drama. This may, however, be a trap. In his resistance to certain persons and emotions, the protagonist may propose a situation and a relationship that are bound to take him the farthest away and spare him from dealing with those unpleasant experiences that have brought him to join a

ACTION

psychodrama group in the first place. If this is the case, the director may need to focus on the resistance, evasion and repression, because the protagonist cannot get anywhere near his primary problem unless such "manoeuvres" and defences are brought to consciousness and processed.

The agreement – or contract – is not a strict requirement; the action may begin with a mere observation of the protagonist's feelings. That which is "here and now" usually leads us into a scene which discloses the feeling the protagonist is experiencing at the moment. The scene usually shows a situation that has recently happened in the protagonist's life. The protagonist sets the scene, arranging objects in space and commenting: "These two chairs will represent a two-seater sofa, and those three, at an angle of 90 degrees, will stand for a three-seater." As such an arrangement of furniture customarily requires a coffee-table, the protagonist adds a small low table, a matchbox functioning as a telephone, a tapestry on the wall symbolizing a photograph of his parents etc. In that way the space is created for an event from the protagonist's life to take place. During the arrangements, the director asks the protagonist a number of questions such as: "What is this?" or "Whose seat is that?" or

"What does that thing there stand for?" etc. Being in the present tense, the questions introduce the protagonist and the director and the group into an "as if" situation. It is "as if" they are witnessing a scene taking place before them. As the next step, the protagonist introduces the "characters" through role reversal and group members are assigned the roles. After this introduction, the scene comes to life, with the dialogue, movements and conduct on the stage exactly following the protagonist's demonstration in the role reversal. The director supports the enactment, monitors the dialogue and movement, appoints the time for role reversal, doubles, and assigns group members as doubles. He observes the protagonist's emotional arousal and seeks to stimulate such a development of action where the protagonist and his feelings may find their fullest expression. He must constantly be aware of himself and his emotions, as well as of the group and its emotions and attitudes. The entire group and the director are helping to facilitate the protagonist's emotional expression. The director's responsibility is to remove, or at least try to remove, anything that may hinder emotional expression. This may include the protagonist's reactions, or tears or shouts within the group, or an auxiliary ego slipping into "a film of his own" or being unable to act out a role. The director tries to ensure that the enactment serves to explain and deepen the protagonist's understanding of the scene, and not just to recount the scene.

After this introductory scene, the psychodramatic action usually moves on to explore situations from the protagonist's recent, distant or even remote past – often

childhood – where the problem presented in the initial scene is traced to its root. Here the emotional charge is often powerful and leads to a catharsis.

The processing of cathartic experience, its concretization, and the disclosure of repressed emotions through the enactment of scenes lead the protagonist towards insight and a new behaviour pattern essential for an adequate resolution of the present-time problem that has been our starting point. This is achieved by taking the protagonist back to the introductory scene with the task to act, now that he is enriched with an insight into the nature of his difficulties, in a way that would enable him to express his attitudes and feelings clearly.

Such a development of psychodramatic action can be illustrated graphically with a psychodramatic spiral, which takes the following course: having obtained the protagonist through the warm-up, we establish the problem. Then we look for a scene that would provide an exposition of the problem –

when, where and with whom did it arise? Through reestablishing the connection with scenes similar in content that took place in the protagonist's recent or distant past, we usually arrive at the **protoscene** for that type of event, the latter being usually hidden in the protagonist's distant past, or in childhood. The release of its emotional charge produces catharsis. Subsequent to the cathartic experience, the conflict scene becomes concretized and integrated through insight. This takes us back to the initial bend of the spiral, but not to the same place. The protagonist

ACTION

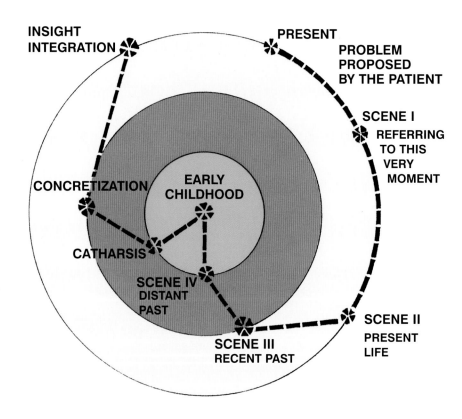

INSIGHT
INTEGRATION

PRESENT

PROBLEM
PROPOSED
BY THE PATIENT

SCENE I
REFERRING
TO THIS
VERY
MOMENT

CONCRETIZATION

EARLY
CHILDHOOD

CATHARSIS

SCENE IV
DISTANT
PAST

SCENE II
PRESENT
LIFE

SCENE III
RECENT PAST

returns to the present through reworking the introductory scene, but now enriched with an awareness of the influence that the past has exerted on his present state.

CLOSURE

Closure is the final scene of a psychodramatic enactment, and is followed by sharing. It constitutes the climax of the drama. It is the moment of becoming aware, of gaining insight, which is accompanied by emotional relief. Not always does the final scene bring the entire process to a closure. At times the sharing elicits in the participants a sense of being relieved from the burden of emotions, a sense of serenity and clarity. It may also happen that the process in the protagonist and his fellow participants does not take place until days after the session. Not infrequently, a psychodrama merely launches the process resulting in an emotional denouement only later, after one or several new dramas. The intrapsychic organization, the establishment of new interrelations of mental representations of objects is a process that may take place anytime after the dramatic enactment.

The first psychodrama example below does not have a happy ending, but it fits in with Moreno's principle of the fulfilment of desire. In this case, it is the fulfilment of an aggressive desire. In the psychodrama, the protagonist acted out her aggressive fantasy and killed her father. The consequence of this aggressive fantasy action is the loss of the bad part of the internal object of the father. In surplus reality, the protagonist compensated for her loss, perceiving the live father's figure and accepting the father as a whole – with his good and his bad parts ("**You make me sick**"). She destroyed the bad parts of her father in fantasy, and repaired them – reintrojected them – in surplus reality in a less bad form. This is likely to result in reduced tension and a more realistic approach to life situations.

CATHARSIS

ROLE REVERSAL

BEHAVIOUR TRAINING

PRESENTATION OF PROBLEM

CHOICE OF PROTAGONIST

RECOGNITION OF RESISTANCES

EXPLORATION OF PROBLEM

SHARING

DISCUSSION

CONCLUSION

INTENSITY OF EMOTIONS

WARM-UP   **ACTION**   **INTEGRATION**

SHARING

Once the psychodramatic action is over, group members take seats in a circle and, facing the protagonist, give an account of how they have experienced his drama. In doing so, they speak about their emotions and their life in the first person. As a matter of fact, they speak about their own life situations summoned by the protagonist's psychodrama. They do not give advice to the protagonist, nor do they analyse his behaviour.

Sharing is the time for group members to convey personal experiences evoked by the protagonist's drama. It is the moment of unity of the group and the protagonist. The group's unity is the moment marked by the fullest individuality of individuals in togetherness. The group's unity is the state of being most our own selves while being together.

PROCESSING

After the psychodrama, the group resumes after a break in order to analyze – or "process" – the director's performance. This phase of a psychodrama session is reserved for educational/training groups. The protagonist's presence is not necessary. If agreed, the processing can be carried out prior to the next group meeting, which may be several days after the drama.

During processing, the participants put forward ideas about the director's work and think about ways in which a scene could have been done better or differently. Of course, different views of the problems that were dealt with in a drama stem from different ways of seeing the protagonist or from different theoretical approaches. Group members always bear in mind that it is not their place to analyze the protagonist but the director's work.

ROLES IN PSYCHODRAMA

The term "role" comes from the Latin word *rotula*. In ancient Greece and Rome, actors listened to their roles being read to them and strove to memorize them through repetition. Originally borrowed from theatre vocabulary, the word has come to be adopted in many sciences pursuing the study of man: philosophy, psychology, sociology, anthropology. "**Man is a role player**", Moreno used to say. His concept of mental health is based on the idea that every personality is made up of a series of roles, and that every person's goal is to develop as wide a repertoire of roles as possible in order to function with full-scale creativity. People who operate within a narrow range of roles, or find it difficult to switch from one role to another, function in their lives in a limited, constrained and insufficiently spontaneous way. In order to be authentic, a role requires spontaneity.

The role is an established pattern of human behaviour. Roles often come in response to another person in a reciprocal role, for example child and parent; student and teacher; doctor and patient. They result from the interaction of child and parent, student and teacher, doctor and patient, leader and the led. Moreno divided roles into: biological, psychological and social.

- Biological roles are unchangeable and related to man's biological functioning: feeding, sleeping, sexual behaviour.
- Psychological roles have their origin in interpersonal relations. At play in these relations are: love, hatred, envy, gratitude, dominance, submissiveness, rivalry, competition, struggle for power.
- Social roles were called cultural conserves by Moreno.

In accordance with its beliefs and conceptions, every culture prescribes the patterns of behaviour appropriate to various social roles: a doctor, politician, teacher, priest, pharmacist, believer, baker. In some cultures, the doctor is a medicine man making use of magic and herbs. In others, however, the doctor is a professional using high technology – computers, X-rays, scanners.

Societies differ. In some societies, the politician is seen as a God-given, powerful and untouchable leader, not as a government official who can be appointed or dismissed.

When we explore and work with the roles, we learn about which roles are repressed, and we uncover unconscious fantasies and emotions that affect our behaviour in certain relationships. It then becomes possible for us to modify our roles and develop more adequate behaviour in our relationships. Every role is dividable into parts. The woman's role may be made up of several sub-roles: mother, daughter, friend, working woman (career-related roles), wife.

To work through the roles may help the repressed parts of our personality manifest themselves.

ROLE ANALYSIS

Role analysis as part of psychodramatic work is a powerful diagnostic means, but it is also an instrument of therapy.

Working through and analyzing the protagonist's roles can provide information for further examination, such as:

• What is the protagonist's leading role?

• Are some roles within the personality suppressed or neglected?

• Does this pose some intrapsychic and interpersonal problems for the protagonist?

• Are some roles overdeveloped at the expense of some other, repressed, ones?

• Are there some needs that remain ungratified because the protagonist has not ventured into certain roles?

The number of investigated possibilities is large. Each role, and each sub-role within a role can obtain their individual graphic representation. Depending on the type of interactions between the person and other people, the person's roles change and undergo modifications.

ROLE REVERSAL

Role reversal is the basic psychodramatic technique. In role reversal the protagonist represents his experience of the significant Others.

In role reversal, the protagonist represents his experience and perception of significant people in his life by taking on their role.

Role reversal provides basic information about the characters in a psychodrama.

Through role reversal our fantasies about ourselves and others come to be unveiled.

"AS IF" SITUATION

A person is least of all himself when he talks as himself. Give him a mask, he will tell the truth.

Oscar Wilde

The "**as if**" situation is a form of symbolic thinking on the stage. It is a form of spontaneity that plays a significant practical role in the process of energizing and integrating one's self. Thus the "**as if**" principle underlies children's games. When such a situation is not functioning no psychodramatic work is possible. The protagonist is encouraged to externalize his internal objects, and it is an "**as if**" situation that creates the opportunity. The director may say: "Now take the role of your father, '**as if**' you were your father now", or: "Dream your dream '**as if**' it were happening now." The "**as if**" situation is a representation, a projection of our mental space towards the outside. All psychodramatic techniques are based on the "**as if**" situation. It is a *conditio sine qua non* for psychodrama.

DOUBLE, DOUBLING

Doubling takes place when a member of the group plays the role of the protagonist. His activity on stage is called doubling. Standing beside or behind the protagonist, the double assumes the same posture, moves the arms and face likewise, and utters the words he empathically feels as belonging to the protagonist and which the latter is presently unaware of or unready to express. The action of copying the protagonist's body attitudes or facial expressions facilitates the double's verbal expression in his position of "as if" being the protagonist. Indirectly, through the non-verbal representation of the protagonist, through feeling-into, the double gets to the meanings of body movements, facial expressions and postures that the protagonist is unaware of. Transposing his experience into words the double complements, discovers concealed meanings, comments, repeats, shows to the protagonist, as if in a mirror, how he sees him.

People often use the technique of doubling in daily life. A girl would spontaneously stiffen her arms and legs to show her brother, a catatonic schizophrenic (mental illness where the sufferer takes strange positions of the body and limbs, or repeats words and movements), how he looks, or how she sees him.

"You look like a candle," she says to her brother and stiffens up. It always makes him laugh, and thereupon he appears to be more relaxed.

Doubling and mirroring and surplus reality, all these are elements of the same process – that of transforming the unconscious into the conscious, of adding to a blinkered consciousness the surplus of reality it has been unable to receive for a number of reasons, repression, social limitations, an influence of the personal and social unconscious.

A traditional healer employs a modified technique of doubling. He says to the patient:

Suggestion, guided fantasy and an empty chair are the techniques that the healer makes use of. He encourages the patient to imagine and visualize his illness as a being, but without using the double, a person or an object that would play the role of the illness.

MIRRORING

Mirroring is a specific group phenomenon. A person can see himself, or an aspect of himself, usually the repressed one, reflected in the behaviour of others as if in a mirror. He can distinguish that others behave just like he does or completely opposite. So he comes to learn what he is like – which is the fundamental process in the ego development – through the influence he exerts on others, and through his image as reflected in their behaviour.

The differentiation of an individual necessitates a shared space. It is only when we see people together, in a group, that we become able to distinguish them in their singularity. Sharing the same space and time, we come to create common attitudes. Being together with others, a person discovers his identity, that which makes him different from others. And at the same time, he builds his own attitude towards the world, a distinctive outlook in a given space and time.

Mirroring may be **benign**, a constructive act of recognizing self in others, and others in self. In that way a new self-image is formed, built on insights into self and self in others.

Negative, **malignant** mirroring is a narrow view of others in whom nothing else is seen but the undesired and ugly, which then is felt as persecutory, disdainful and wrong.

As Narcissus dies without having received the echo of presence from his own, unrecognized, image in the mirror of a pool, a group member falls seriously ill if his emotions and needs fail to be echoed back by the destructive mirror of the group.

In the process of mirroring, a constructive act of the presence and grace of the **Other** in a group, the **Encounter**, being in-between and a dialog occur, and my self becomes **I** and yours becomes **You**.

Mirroring is also a psychodramatic technique. The protagonist chooses his double from among group members, and standing aside watches a scene being enacted by the group members in the roles of the significant Others (auxiliary egos) and himself (the double). Thus he concretizes the role of the observing aspect of his self (observing ego) and, taking a side-view of a life situation of his, gains concrete insights into his behaviour "as if" watching himself in a mirror. Employed as a psychodramatic technique, mirroring permits the protagonist to take part in his scene as an observer, rather than as a participant immersed in emotions and interpersonal relations that hinder him from viewing his situation in its entirety.

SURPLUS REALITY

Surplus reality is part of psychic reality, an unrecognizable dimension of reality. The surplus includes all that has been pushed aside, repressed, fantasized, desired but unattained. As a psychodramatic technique, surplus reality is the concretization of the possible, of what did not happen but could have, or is not happening but might. It is closely related to the desire principle.

TELE IN PSYCHODRAMA

Tele is a term of Greek origin, literally meaning – at a distance. Moreno borrowed it from Greek drama and tragedy where it had been used to describe feelings arising between the audience and the actor – at a distance. The audience is watching the tragedy and feeling into the hero's suffering. The actor, sensing that kind of "energy" emanating from the audience, acts with more authenticity and enthusiasm. This silent exchange between the two forms the basis of telic communication. Tele is contact at a distance enabling an exchange of emotional messages. It is the basic unit of emotion transmitted from one person to another. The meaning of the concept as understood by Moreno includes a very wide range of interpersonal aspects. Contrary to the psychoanalytical concept of transference, tele cannot be used for explaining the repetition of the past in the present, but solely as a relation referring to here and now. Moreno's definition of tele postulates it as a unit of affective energy transmitted from one person to another. Tele is the ability to recognize self in the other and vice versa, as well as the ability to make out the feelings of the other, and the awareness of togetherness thus created. Tele involves: **intuition**, **empathy** and **transference**. Tele is a cognitive-connate-affective relationship between people. The philosopher Martin Buber defines the relationship to the other as being in-between. Only through an **encounter** that is free from desire, interest and purpose do we become authentic beings, **I** and **you**.

SPONTANEITY

The word draws its origin from the Latin word *sua sponte* – free will. To behave spontaneously means to act instantaneously and on impulse. Spontaneity is a prerequisite for creativity. The two terms stand in a twin-relation and are mutually dependent. There is no creativity without spontaneity and vice versa. Spontaneity is the released creative energy. Reflex and instinctive actions are spontaneous. Children are spontaneous, and adults may be spontaneous when they feel no fear. The duality of spontaneity and creativity differs from impulsive behaviour or automatic spontaneity, the latter being neglectful of a more profound meaning of spontaneity and reducing it to something uncontrolled and typical of animal behaviour.

CREATIVITY

Creativity is the process of creating, an energy released for creating new interpersonal relations, new modes of behaviour, works of art and science. Creativity is a novel expression of man's spontaneous needs. It is the ability to create new relations and an expression of man's spontaneity. It is the creation of new connections between man's spontaneous needs. Creativity is the process of transformation (change) of man's drives, needs and impulses into a novel expression (work of art). Creativity is the sublimation of instinctual energy.

TEMPORAL UNIVERSALS

They are defined by the Aristotelian principle of unity of action, time and space that is applied both in theatre and in psychodrama. The basic questions posed by psychodrama are: who, when and where. The answers lead us back to the beginning of the protagonist's drama that takes place in the "timeless unconscious". In feelings, unfinished thoughts and actions, and intuitions, the director and the group discover the protagonist's hidden world.

CATHARSIS

C atharsis is a very old concept, taken over from Aristotle. He first refers to it in his *Poetics* when speaking about the effect of Greek tragedy on the audience. Aristotle distinguishes the aesthetic and ethical effects of catharsis. In terms of psychoanalysis, catharsis is a release from tension and anxiety by way of reliving past experiences, especially those that were repressed as unpleasant, unacceptable and traumatic to the patient. As theatre spectators, we watch the actors on stage passively. They may arouse us to some emotions that may or may not have something to do with us and our lives. Consequently, the catharsis experienced by a theatre audience is secondary and passive. In psychodrama, in an "as if" situation, the protagonist re-enacts scenes from his own life, and often lets out for the first time the emotions he was unaware of, or could not or dared not show. In psychodrama, this is called mental catharsis. It brings about change starting from the inside. Each mental catharsis Is specific, unique and unrepeatable for it is related to a specific problem.

The cathartic experience is followed by the protagonist's return to reality, to the present, accompanied by an integration of the experience gained in the previous psychodramatic action and of the emotions brought out by mental catharsis. A person may not be aware of the significance that the released emotion may have to him. It is acceptable to speak about mental catharsis in case that such a release of emotion is associated with the protagonist's insight into the origin and meaning of the emotion. The importance of mental catharsis as a therapeutic factor, that which brings about change in psychodramatic work, has often been emphasized. Emotional discharge, however, is not in itself the goal of psychodrama, nor is catharsis the only important factor.

THERAPEUTIC FACTORS

I rvin D. Yalom, a leading theoretician of group therapy, has postulated eleven therapeutic factors included to a lesser or greater extent in every group therapeutic approach. **Therapeutic factors are elements that, either in isolation or (especially) in association, produce a therapeutic effect in man.**

- installation of hope
- universality
- imparting information
- altruism
- corrective recapitulation of the primary family group
- development of socializing techniques
- imitative behaviour
- interpersonal learning
- group cohesiveness
- catharsis
- existential factors

The most relevant to psychodrama are: group cohesiveness; imitative behaviour (through role play); development of socializing techniques, achieved by way of continuously working through roles; existential factors; and, last but not least, catharsis.

PSYCHODRAMA EXAMPLE 1

29

30

PROTAGONIST INTRODUCES
HER BOYFRIEND

PROTAGONIST CHOOSES A MEMBER FOR
THE ROLE OF HER BOYFRIEND

SCENE WITH PROTAGONIST
AND HER BOYFRIEND
IS SET

SCENE
PROGRESSES

PROTAGONIST POINTS
TO HER GROIN

DIRECTOR REQUESTS
ROLE REVERSAL

PROTAGONIST
IN THE ROLE
OF AUXILIARY EGO

WHOLE SCENE
WITH THE BOYFRIEND
IS ACTED OUT...

PROTAGONIST TURNS TO THERAPIST

PROTAGONIST AND AUXILIARY EGO PROCEED WITH PSYCHODRAMA

SOLILOQUY (PROTAGONIST'S MONOLOGUE)

DAUGHTER IS 21 YEARS OLD

32

33

PROTAGONIST IN THE ROLE OF HER FATHER

38

40

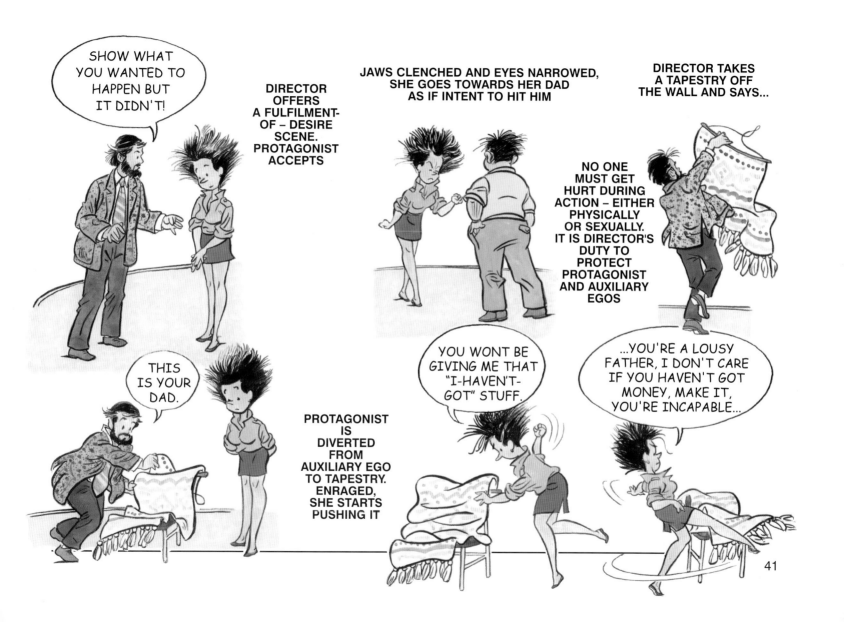

THIS HAS NEVER REALLY HAPPENED, WE'VE SEEN A FANTASY.* FATHER AND MOTHER ARE HERE, AT HOME! TO END WITH...

AFTER THIS SCENE THAT DIDN'T HAPPEN IN REAL LIFE, THE ONE WHERE FATHER PERISHES, IS THERE...

...ANY MESSAGE FOR YOUR PARENTS?

*SURPLUS REALITY, AN UNRECOGNIZED PART OF REALITY, EFFECTUAL FANTASY, TO A GREAT EXTENT UNCONSCIOUS

NEW SCENE IS OFFERED AS THE DRAMATIC ACTION CLOSURE SURPLUS REALITY. PROTAGONIST HAS AN OPPORTUNITY TO SAY OR DO SOMETHING SHE HAS NEVER DONE OR SAID BEFORE

WHAT WOULD YOU TELL THEM?

YOU MAKE ME SICK!

PARENTS SIT NEXT TO EACH OTHER, AS A COUPLE

PROTAGONIST LOOKS AT THEM SCORNFULLY

PROTAGONIST TURNS HER BACK TO THEM

43

SHARING

ONCE A PSYCHODRAMA ENDS, PROTAGONIST, DIRECTOR AND AUXILIARY EGOS LEAVE THE STAGE AND TAKE THEIR SEATS IN A CIRCLE

SHARING REFERS TO THE SHARING OF FEELINGS. WHEN PSYCHODRAMATIC ACTION ENDS, GROUP MEMBERS SIT DOWN IN A CIRCLE AND TELL THE PROTAGONIST WHAT HIS/HER DRAMA HAS ELICITED IN THEM. THEY SPEAK ABOUT THEIR FEELINGS AND EVENTS FROM THEIR LIVES. THEY SHARE THEIR EXPERIENCE WITH THE PROTAGONIST AND THE GROUP.

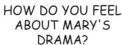

HOW DO YOU FEEL ABOUT MARY'S DRAMA?

I HAVE CONFLICTS WITH MY MOTHER. I CAN NEVER EXPRESS FULLY WHAT I FEEL. SHE ALWAYS KNOWS BEST, KEEPS CONTROLLING ME, WHILE I HOLD BACK, KEEP QUIET, DON'T HAVE GUTS!

I ENVY YOUR HAVING DONE THIS, I SHOULD'VE DONE THE SAME TO MY FATHER, SUCH A WEAKLING! HE NEVER UNDERSTOOD ME. SUFFOCATED ME ALL THE TIME, NEVER GAVE ME ANY MONEY OR LOVE OR PROTECTION.

I DON'T KNOW IF THIS IS RELATED IN ANY WAY... I ALWAYS LOVED IT WHEN MY FATHER, COMING BACK FROM TRIPS, GAVE ME CHOCOLATES FROM DIFFERENT COUNTRIES. ONCE HE WAS ON A LONG TRIP, AND I REALLY WANTED THE CHOCOLATES.

WHEN HE CAME BACK, I REALIZED THAT HE HAD FORGOTTEN TO BRING ME ANY. I FELT AWFUL. VERY DISAPPOINTED...

...I COULDN'T UNDERSTAND. MY DAD NOT GIVING ME WHAT I LOVE THE MOST. AND I LOVE HIM SO MUCH!

THE PSYCHODRAMA IS OVER!

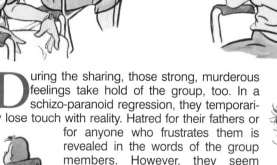

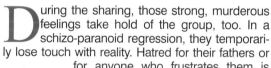

During the sharing, those strong, murderous feelings take hold of the group, too. In a schizo-paranoid regression, they temporarily lose touch with reality. Hatred for their fathers or for anyone who frustrates them is revealed in the words of the group members. However, they seem unaware of the hatred, as if they had not just witnessed a murder on stage as the realization of a fantasy of destruction.

Only one of them is sad, remembering that she was denied her favourite sweets by her father. She neither hates not fantasizes about killing. She feels sad because those closest to us are not so committed as to fulfill our every wish. Within the group, she is a depressively positioned islet of maturity and integration.

DEVELOPMENT OF PSYCHODRAMA

- There was no warm-up for this drama

- An element of integration shows during the sharing as sorrow over unobtained love from dad – father's sweets

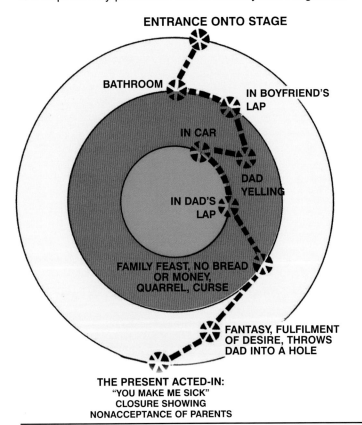

ENTRANCE ONTO STAGE

BATHROOM

IN BOYFRIEND'S LAP

IN CAR

DAD YELLING

IN DAD'S LAP

FAMILY FEAST, NO BREAD OR MONEY, QUARREL, CURSE

FANTASY, FULFILMENT OF DESIRE, THROWS DAD INTO A HOLE

THE PRESENT ACTED-IN:
"YOU MAKE ME SICK"
CLOSURE SHOWING
NONACCEPTANCE OF PARENTS

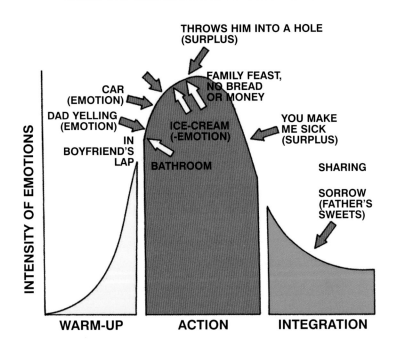

INTENSITY OF EMOTIONS

THROWS HIM INTO A HOLE (SURPLUS)

CAR (EMOTION)

FAMILY FEAST, NO BREAD OR MONEY

DAD YELLING (EMOTION)

ICE-CREAM (-EMOTION)

YOU MAKE ME SICK (SURPLUS)

IN BOYFRIEND'S LAP

BATHROOM

SHARING

SORROW (FATHER'S SWEETS)

WARM-UP **ACTION** **INTEGRATION**

DIRECTOR'S COMMENTARY ON KEY WORDS

PERIOD The protagonist is happy that she is having her period. She makes use of it as part of a love game. She gestures towards her lower belly and says, "You'll be a dad." She uses the lie playfully, to stimulate sexual desire.

In surplus reality, a particular and insufficiently recognized dimension of reality, the moment her menstruation occurs is the moment she faces emotions. Failing her menstruation, a woman may be happy, sad, scared, desperate, perplexed, exultant. When it occurs, men usually say: "Well, fine", unaware of the emotional significance the occurrence has for women.

Menstruation is an event marking the initiation that turns a girl into a woman. It introduces a rhythm, a cyclic change in the emotional and corporeal functioning. With its cessation, a rhythm dies out.

If they are uninformed, when their first menstruation occurs girls are often scared, believing they are sick and are going to die. In traditional culture, menstruation is magically associated with impurity and uncleanness.

Failure to inform girls about menstruation is a form of their psychological castration.

OEDIPAL SITUATION From an encounter between a man and a woman a child is born. The mother, child and father form a triangle, a triangular situation.

Emotions and knowledge that arise in the triangle between the mum, dad and child constitute a basis for a person's relations with others. Our whole life is marked by a variety of triangular situations: two women and a man; two men and a woman; a student, father and professor; a mum, child and teacher; an employer, employee and husband or wife; a therapist, group and protagonist. Children find it difficult to function in threesomes. Two, four or five kids pose no problem, but a three-way communication is always difficult: one must fall out. Two women come to blows when a man appears between them. A man may lose his best friend when one of them falls in love.

In this psychodrama, she's having a shower, her father knocks on the door. She spots her menstrual blood, which means: "Nothing has happened." It helps relieve the tension in the triangle between her, her boyfriend and her father.

INCEST Incest is sexual contact between closely related people. Sexual attraction between family members, which may or may not reach the point of realiza-tion, is a form of incestuous behaviour. It is often difficult to tell whether an incestuous story is a figment of imagination or it actually happened. Our experience of the Oedipal situation provides a basis for our attitude towards the opposite sex, i.e. we are shaping it on the model of our attitude towards our parent of the opposite sex. Our parent of the same sex is our rival and a model for us to identify with. Without being able to define one's self in the presence of the parent of the opposite sex, one can never feel complete. Hence the importance of both the mother and father to a daughter, and of both the father and mother to a son.

ENJOYMENT For a little girl, sitting in her father's lap and feeling special and loved can bring a great feeling of enjoyment and security. She feels as though she means everything in the world to him. If Mum is also there, the girl may think to herself, "I'm more important to him than you are."

FULFILMENT OF DESIRE Fulfilment of desire is a basic principle of Moreno's psychodrama. In psychodrama, the fulfilment of desire, or a fantasy about fulfilment of desire, reveals our true nature. We often say a thing is, while it is actually a thing wished for but not happening. As a result, others think we're making things up, and we are unhappy.

We wish to love someone, to be loved, to be happy, highly regarded, but we also may wish to hurt someone and cause him harm. The extent to which we manage to get, or come close to getting, what we wish for, is a measure of our feeling well. The extent to which we fail to get what we wish for is a measure of our not feeling well.

LOVE First mum and dad have met each other and then we are born. Meeting – and the Book of Genesis says: "Adam lay with his wife Eve, and she became pregnant and gave birth to Cain. She said, 'With the help of the Lord I have brought forth a man.'" – is the moment of creation.

Love is: getting together, creation, belonging, giving, nourishment, protection, safety, desire and fulfilment of desire, sitting in dad's lap, participation, presence, acceptance, being with the Other.

Love is to believe, not a make-believe, not "as if". Love is truth. "As if" is a search for love, for encounter, for closeness, a movement towards truth.

SORROW Sorrow is the feeling of loss of a beloved person.

We express sorrow over an unrequited love.

And at not getting all we need from the one we love.

The acceptance of the fact that we cannot get all we want from the object of our love puts us in a depressive position.

If we are able not to hate the one we love despite being denied what we want, we are in a depressive position.

A depressive position is a prerequisite for maturity.

CURSE Acting out the role of the father, the protagonist says, "You're a whore!", laying an emphasis on the target as if uncertain where it might be.

According to Donald Meltzer, our psychosexual development includes an early phase of confusion about body zones, in which sources of sexual pleasure are distributed all over the body. Through further development and maturing, sexual impulses centre around the genital areas.

A cursing man regresses from the level of mature sexuality to a state of infantile polymorphous perversity, the whole body becoming a target for his sexual or aggressive excitement. In such a state of regression, the aggressive and the sexual are not separated. Hence, the primary meaning of the curse is that of an act of aggression.

GREED Omnipotent oral fantasy. The greedy cannot have enough, they always want more. They are always unhappy because they constantly feel they have little.

Children are greedy. As a child, our protagonist wished for loads of ice-cream.

As an adult, she wishes to get a suit, but the suppressed energy of her infantile greed makes her oversensitive to frustration induced by her father's words: "Haven't got the money." Hence she responds with anger. Greed inhibits rational thinking and the reality principle.

CONFLICT An encounter of opposite feelings. I want – I want not, It's OK – It's not OK, I will – I won't, I like – I like not, I have – I have not. Such words are always accompanied by strong emotions. Family members love and hate, attract and repel each other. Our desires are often in conflict with what our family is able to offer. As a result, we repress them, thereby provoking an internal conflict between our desires, as fantasies about satisfying our instinctual needs, and the possibilities offered in reality.

This drama involves a conflict between the protagonist's wish to have much money in order to fulfil her desires and the reality principle expressed by the parental reply: "I don't have money."

There is yet another conflict in this drama, that between her yearning for unconditional parental love, which gives as much ice-cream as we want, and the realistic attitude of the adults that seems to convey the message: money first, then love, or duty first, then pleasure. As the poet Zmaj said in one of his poems for children: "Work first, then play."

MONEY Money is a means of communication between our desires and reality. If a girl has a strong wish to get herself a suit, she has to have the money to fulfil it. It may happen that we identify money with the fulfilment of wishes. Then money becomes a symbol, and people say: "If you have money, you can have everything."

If you have money, it is "as if" you had everything: love, happiness, power.

Money is a neurotic symbol. When we strongly wish for something, we put tremendous energy into making the money to fulfil the wish. But money is not: love, happiness, health, safety. Money is a substitute. To have money means "as if" having love, health, safety.

HATRED Hatred is the dominance of the aggressive over the libidinal. We express hatred with a blow, an abrupt movement, rude words, a threatening look, yells, curses. We hate when we are helpless and not getting what we want. Not only does the protagonist in this drama not get her suit, she does not even get fresh bread. Her parents seem to be saying: "You're good for nothing. Not even for fresh bread. Stale bread, that's what you're good for." Hurt, she responds with hatred. She is striking blows, yelling, throwing her father into a hole, invoking dark underground forces. A blow is an ambivalent act. On the one hand, it is a desire to destroy the object of one's hatred as well as one's attitude towards it. On the other hand, buried under the noise of the aggression, a violent blow is also a desire for fusion, a desire to unite in touch, and for the preservation of the object's good parts. (This is similar to the proverbial "cold hands, warm heart.")

ENVY Envy originates in the dual relationship between the mother and the child. We grow envious of someone who has something we need but do not have. Mum has Dad, and the child must wait for an opportunity to play with Dad. Mum and Dad have fresh bread for the family feast, and the money to buy her a suit if they want to. The protagonist hasn't got the power to decide and, feeling helpless, she grows envious. In a scene of this drama, the parents have bought plenty of food but won't give any of it to their daughter, just as they won't give her the money to buy a suit. The way she feels it, they aren't giving her anything.

CONTROL It is in others that we often find the reason for feeling bad. We believe that the bad in us comes from others, unaware that we are attributing our own bad to them because we are unable to cope with it by ourselves. What we achieve by doing so is that the bad – hatred, envy, malice – remain under control, being unconsciously transferred from within us into others and recognized as belonging to others, not to us.

During the sharing, when a member of the group says about the mother: "She always knows best, controlling me all the time", it is as if she said: "She keeps saying I'm not good", which means: "It is really me thinking that she is not good."

FATHER'S SWEETS Father's sweets are delicious and are associated with this group member's love for her father. When her father comes back from his trips, he gives her what she likes best – the sweets. When he fails to give his child her favourite food, she feels that her dad doesn't love her. This is why she is sad.

ACTING OUT Acting out is a poorly controlled action. Strong feelings often take a shorter way out without having been processed consciously. Acting out is: an accidentally broken glass, a forgotten birthday, a clumsily spilt drink, an outburst of anger out of proportion to its immediate cause.

Acting out in this drama is also the anger and physical aggression against the father.

PATRICIDE According to Freud, patricide is at the beginning of civilization. The guilt that sons of the horde felt after having killed their father made them establish a set of rules of conduct in a group. Thus social hierarchy was created. Emotions shown by the protagonist in this drama are strong and wild, as though from the times of the primitive horde. Patricide is part of an "as if" situation in the drama. It stimulates group members in the sharing to speak about their feelings, love and hate for their parents.

PSYCHODRAMA EXAMPLE 2

I'D LIKE TO WORK TODAY.

PROCESSING – FOURTH PART OF A PSYCHODRAMATIC SESSION, RESERVED FOR EDUCATIONAL/TRAINING GROUPS, TAKES PLACE AFTER THE SHARING. ITS PURPOSE: TO DISCUSS THE DIRECTION OF THE DRAMA

TEN MINUTES' BREAK ALWAYS FOLLOWS PROCESSING IN ORDER TO SEPARATE TWO PHASES OF WORK

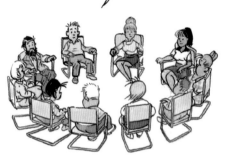

GROUP MEMBERS SIT IN A CIRCLE, SILENT, SMILING...

DO YOU KNOW ON WHAT?

I'D WORK THROUGH SOME PROBLEMS AT WORK.

SOME GROUPS ARE MANAGED BY A CO-THERAPEUTIC COUPLE. CLIENTS IN THERAPEUTIC GROUPS HAVE A CHOICE OF TWO DIRECTORS. IN EDUCATIONAL/ TRAINING GROUPS ALL MEMBERS ARE POTENTIAL DIRECTORS

I WANT TO WORK WITH YOU!

OK.

53

54

55

59

63

ANA IN ANDREW'S ROLE

73

A GLOSSARY OF PSYCHODRAMATIC TERMS AND TECHNIQUES

ACTION – Physical movement. Doing something. Part of a psychodramatic session.

AXIODRAMA – Utilization of psychodramatic techniques with the aim of illuminating religious, ethical and cultural issues.

AUTODRAMA – Session in which the protagonist functions as his own director.

AUXILIARY EGO – The "significant Other"; a member of the group chosen by the protagonist for the role of an important person in his life (father, wife, employer etc).

CATHARSIS – Purification and release of emotions (e.g. anger, fear etc).

CREATIVITY – The finding or discovering of new modes of thought and behaviour.

DIRECTOR – A therapist and the person who leads the psychodrama.

DIRECTOR AS THE DOUBLE – The director may double if necessary, but needs to quickly step out of the role in order to resume the directing of the drama.

DIRECTOR, HIS OBJECTIVITY – The director remains objective regardless of the emotionality of dramatic "material".

DOUBLES, DOUBLING – "Feeling into" the role of the protagonist: copying the posture of his body, movements and facial expressions in order to say the words and make the movements the double feels to be "right" for a given situation, which, however, the protagonist is unable to see as such at the moment. While in action, the double usually stands behind or beside the protagonist. After the double's action, the director asks the protagonist: Are those your words? Would you have done the same? The protagonist's acceptance or refusal of the double's action stimulates the development of psychodramatic action.

DREAM PRESENTATION – The protagonist positions himself in the space and time he usually goes to bed, takes the appropriate posture, recreates the atmosphere of his "bedroom". Auxiliary egos play the roles of significant persons and objects from the protagonist's dream.

ECHO – The director repeats the protagonist's words, like an echo, as if they had been spoken too quietly to be heard by the group.

FAMILY PSYCHODRAMA – Psychodrama involving members of a family playing themselves.

FREEZE – Stoppage of the action: when the protagonist is overheated, when the director wants to regain control etc. The action is stopped by the director.

GUIDED FANTASY – A method of warming up: the director invites the group or the protagonist to imagine themselves in a fantasy situation (journey through space, rebirth, being "in someone else's shoes", someone significant, etc).

MIRRORING – Auxiliary egos replay the scenes and actions in which the protagonist took part. The protagonist observes, as if in a mirror, "himself" and others in action.

NON-VERBAL COMMUNICATION – The director draws attention to postures of the body, tone of voice, movement, facial expression etc.

PROTAGONIST – The principal "character" in a psychodrama. The person whose conflict is being elucidated on stage.

PROJECTION OF THE FUTURE – The protagonist chooses a scene he expects might happen, and he also chooses the time, place, people.

PSYCHODRAMA A DEUX – Psychodrama in which only the protagonist and the director take part.

PSYCHODRAMATIC ROLES – Mother, father, hero, boss - "the significant Other".

ROLE-PLAYING – The substratum of psychodrama. Search for alternatives, experimentation with new situations, decision-making, training in social skills.

SOCIODRAMA – Psychodramatic action concerned with resolving a problem of interest for the entire group. The characters are not personalized: the teacher, the leader and people, students, the parent and child.

SOCIOGRAM – Sociometric diagram: plotting interpersonal relations within a group.

> **ACTION SOCIOGRAM** – Symbolic presentation of the protagonist's social atom, most often his family. Characters are arranged in such a way that the space, bodies, facial expressions and their messages suggest the family dynamics.

SOLILOQUY – Verbalization of the protagonist's thoughts and feelings (protagonist's monologue).

STRUCTURED WARM-UP – Warm-up for finding the protagonist: an empty chair, magic shop, photograph.

SURPLUS REALITY – An extra dimension of reality, "larger than reality". In fact, the recuperation of a possible dimension of reality, people, events, objects.

SPONTANEITY TRAINING – Training and rehearsal of new roles in new situations with the aim of developing spontaneity.

VIGNETTE – A short psychodramatic work. Usually a single scene or tableau.

WARM-UP – Tasks that the director assigns to the group in order to obtain several protagonists. The beginning of a psychodramatic session.

RECOMMENDED READING

Blatner, A. (1997) *Acting-In: Practical Applications of Psychodramatic Methods* (3rd edition). London: Free Association Books.

Blatner, A. with Blatner, A. (1988) *Foundations of Psychodrama: History, Theory and Practice* (3rd edition). New York: Springer Publishing Company.

Fonseca, J. (2004) *Contemporary Psychodrama: New Approaches to Theory and Technique*. Hove: Brunner-Routledge.

Fox, J. (Ed.) (1987) *The Essential Moreno: Writings on Psychodrama, Group Methods and Spontaneity*. New York: Springer.

Holmes, P. and Karp, M. (Eds.) (1991) *Psychodrama: Inspiration and Technique*. London: Tavistock/Routledge.

Holmes, P., Karp, M. and Watson, M. (Eds.) (1994) *Psychodrama Since Moreno: Innovations in Theory and Practice*. London: Routledge.

Karp, M., Holmes, P. and Bradshaw Tauvon, K. (Eds.) (1998) *The Handbook of Psychodrama*. London: Tavistock/Routledge.

Kellerman, P.F. (1992) *Focus on Psychodrama: The Therapeutic Aspects of Psychodrama*. London: Jessica Kingsley Publishers.

Kellerman, P.F. and Hudgins, M.K. (Eds.) (2000) *Psychodrama with Trauma Survivors: Acting Out Your Pain*. London: Jessica Kingsley Publishers.

Moreno, J.L. (1985) *Psychodrama: Volume One*. New York: Beacon House. Originally published 1946.

Moreno, J.L. (1993) *Who Shall Survive? Foundations of Sociometry, Group Psychotherapy and Sociodrama*. McLean, Virginia: American Society of Group Psychotherapy and Psychodrama. Published through: Roanoke, Virginia: Royal Publishing Company. Student edition.

Moreno, Z.T., Blomkvist, L. and Rutzel, T. (2000) *Psychodrama, Surplus Reality and the Art of Healing*. London: Routledge.

Pines, M. (1998) *Circular Reflections: Selected Papers on Group Analysis and Psychoanalysis*. London: Jessica Kingsley Publishers.

Schutzenberger, A.A. (1998) *The Ancestor Syndrome*. London: Routledge.

USEFUL ORGANIZATIONS

www.psychodrama.org.uk
Website of the British Psychodrama Association

www.asgpp.org
Website of the American Society of Group Psychotherapy and Psychodrama

www.anzpa.org
Website of the Australia and New Zealand Psychodrama Association

http://members.tripod.com/~portaroma/fepto.htm
Website of the Federation of European Psychodrama Training Organisations Association